**Quick Start (**

The Essential
BLOOD SUGAR
DIET
15 Minute Meals

A Quick Start Guide
To Cooking Quick
Easy Meals
On The

Blood Sugar Diet

Over 80 Calorie Counted Recipes To Lose Weight
And Rebalance Your Body

First published in 2016 by Erin Rose Publishing

Text and illustration copyright © 2016 Erin Rose Publishing

Design: Julie Anson

ISBN: 978-1-911492-03-0

A CIP record for this book is available from the British Library.

DISCLAIMER: This book is for informational purposes only and not intended as a substitute for the medical advice, diagnosis or treatment of a physician or qualified healthcare provider. The reader should consult a physician before undertaking a new health care regime and in all matters relating to his/her health, and particularly with respect to any symptoms that may require diagnosis or medical attention.

While every care has been taken in compiling the recipes for this book we cannot accept responsibility for any problems which arise as a result of preparing one of the recipes. The author and publisher disclaim responsibility for any adverse effects that may arise from the use or application of the recipes in this book. Some of the recipes in this book include nuts and eggs. If you have an egg or nut allergy it's important to avoid these.

CONTENTS

Recipes

LUNCH

DINNER

INTRODUCTION

If you are following the Blood Sugar Diet and need some quick, healthy recipe ideas that fit into your busy lifestyle, then look no further!

Even if you're short on time you can still make delicious, mouth-watering foods which will help you balance your blood sugar, lose weight and make optimum health a reality.

Sugar-free eating is a beneficial for everyone who wants to improve their health and maintain a healthy weight but taking this further and reducing your intake of starchy carbohydrates which can exacerbate blood sugar imbalances means you can maximise healthy eating. Cooking meals and snacks which help to balance your blood sugar can be easier than you thought!

In this Quick Start Guide we bring you plenty of blood sugar friendly recipes for every meal of the day which are sugar-free, low in starches and carbohydrates and leave you feeling satisfied.

All of the recipes and information in this book is clear and concise, making it easy for you to incorporate into your lifestyle. There are so many fast and tasty recipes to choose from you can add variety into your diet without spending too much time in the kitchen. If you are ready to improve your health, read on!

Who Can Benefit?

Every time we eat, our blood sugar levels rise as a result of the food we've just eaten. Sugars and carbohydrates stimulate changes to our blood sugar and insulin levels, causing peaks and troughs which can alter our health and wellbeing both in the short and long term. The effects of excess sugar are well known yet with so many of our foods containing hidden sugars, we are unwittingly eating much more than ever before.

High blood sugar levels and dramatic changes in our blood sugar levels can be avoided by reducing our intake of sugars and carbohydrates including the hidden sugars we're often not aware of.

When you think of blood sugar issues we tend to think of type 2 diabetes as the main target but if you or someone you know has been diagnosed as pre-diabetic, hypoglycaemic, obese or has metabolic syndrome (also known as Syndrome X) and insulin resistance where you have difficulty losing weight, these are signs your body would benefit from better management and improvement in your blood sugar levels.

You must always seek the advice of your doctor for any of these issues and when in doubt make sure there are no underlying conditions.

Below is a brief overview of some of the ways your blood sugar may be affecting your health and lifestyle.

- Finding it difficult to lose any weight, despite your best efforts.
- Anxiety, foggy thinking, irritability, mood swings, brain fog, restlessness, poor concentration and insomnia.
- Excessive tiredness and weakness.
- Desire and cravings for stimulants such as chocolate, sugar, alcohol and caffeine.
- Dizziness, visual disturbances and shakiness.
- High cholesterol and heart disease.

Reducing your sugar intake is beneficial to most people however always check with your medical advisor or doctor before embarking on any radical dietary changes , especially if you are diabetic or are on medication which may need to be monitored or adjusted.

What Can't I Eat?

Below is a list of the food to AVOID.

Sugars

Avoid products containing sugar, such as:

- Chocolate bars, desserts, ice-creams, puddings, sweets and candy.

- Avoid honey, syrup, treacle, maple syrup and agave syrup.

- Marinades and ready-made sauces like sweet chilli sauces, ketchup, barbecue sauce and any dressing containing sugar. Always check the label for added sugar.

- Avoid ripe tropical fruit such as mango and papaya and dried fruit, like apricots, sultanas, raisins and figs.

Carbohydrates

Avoid all starchy carbohydrates such as:

- Bread
- Cakes
- Cereals
- Cookies
- Crackers
- Millet
- Muesli
- Noodles
- Oats
- Pasta
- Potatoes
- Sweet Potatoes
- Rice

Drinks

- Steer clear of beer, wine, spirits, cordials, fruit juices, milk shakes, fizzy drinks, hot chocolates, oat milk and rice milk.

Fats

- Vegetables oils such as corn and canola

- Spreads and margarines which are low fat, contain trans fats or contain sugar.

What Can I Eat?

Below is a list of foods you CAN eat.

- All meats including beef, chicken, lamb, pork and turkey. Avoid breaded and battered meat products.

- Fresh fish such as tuna, haddock, cod, anchovies, salmon, trout, sardines, herring and sole. Shellfish such as prawns, mussels and crab. Avoid breaded or battered fish products.

- Eggs

- Tofu

- Nuts inc. peanut butter, cashew butter and almond butter.

- Seeds

- Beans and pulses such as kidney beans, butter beans, chickpeas (garbanzo beans), pinto beans, cannellini beans, soy beans and lentils.

Fats & Dairy Products

- Butter

- Coconut Oil

- Olive Oil

- Ghee

- Full-fat dairy produce; cheeses, Greek yogurt, sour cream, clotted cream, mascarpone, crème fraîche, fresh cream.

Fruit – Maximum 2 pieces of low sugar fruit per day

- Apples

- Apricots

- Bananas
- Blackberries
- Blackcurrants
- Blueberries
- Cherries
- Grapefruit
- Kiwi
- Kumquat
- Lemons
- Limes
- Melon
- Oranges
- Peaches
- Pears
- Plums
- Pomegranate
- Raspberries
- Redcurrants
- Strawberries

Vegetables

- Avocados
- Asparagus
- Aubergine (Eggplant)
- Bean sprouts
- Broccoli
- Broad Beans
- Brussels Sprouts
- Cabbage
- Cauliflower
- Celery
- Courgette (Zucchini)
- Cucumber
- Kale
- Leeks
- Lettuce
- Mushrooms
- Pak Choi (Bok Choy)
- Peppers (Bell Peppers)

- Radish

- Root veg; such as parsnips, beet-roots and carrots, in moderation as they have a higher carbohydrate content.

- Runner Beans

- Spinach

- Spring Onions (Scallions)

- Olives

- Onions

- Rocket (Arugula)

- Watercress

Drinks

- Tea

- Coffee

- Green Tea

- Water

- Almond Milk

- Soya Milk

Dressings & Condiments

- Fresh herbs

- Lemon juice

- Lime juice

- Spices

- Salt

How To Get Started

Depending on if your goals are to maintain an already healthy weight while improving your blood sugars or if your main target is to lose unwanted weight, you can use the recipes in this book to achieve this. By following the blood sugar diet, you can do both. No matter which option you choose, stick to avoiding the foods on the 'avoid' list and eat from the list of foods you can eat. If your focus is increased weight loss, you can restrict your daily calorie intake to shed those extra pounds.

For those wishing to restrict their calorie intake to improve weight loss, aim to consume no more than 1000 calories per day or less.

The main thing you have to remember is to steer clear of all types of sugar, especially those added to everyday foods and reduce your carbohydrate intake in the form of bread, pasta, rice and potatoes. If this seems overwhelming to begin with you can start off by gradually implementing the changes.

What To Expect

So, let's not sugar coat this. To begin with, you may experience cravings but once you've cut out all the sugars and reduced the carbs they will disappear in a short period of time. Just don't be tempted to stray too far as a sneaky chocolate bar, biscuit or cake can start off the cravings again as it stimulates your blood sugar. However, just get back on track and within a day or two you should be feeling in control again.

Tracking Down The Hidden Sugars

Steering clear of sugar-laden desserts and cakes is essential but so many savoury everyday foods like sausages, marinated and coated meats, soups and baked beans have sugar added to them. The amount of sugars in these foods quickly mounts up. Sugar may not be obviously listed but the ingredients but can be listed under the following names. Avoid these masked sugars.

Agave nectar	Fructose corn syrup
Barley malt	Fructose syrup
Beet sugar	Glucose
Brown sugar	Glucose syrup
Cane juice crystals	Golden syrup
Caramel	Invert sugar syrup
Carob syrup	Malt syrup
Coconut sugar	Maltodextrin
Corn syrup and high fructose corn syrup	Maple syrup
Date syrup	Malt syrup
Dehydrated fruit juice	Molasses
Dextrin	Palm sugar
Dextrose	Refiner's syrup
Ethylmaltol	Sucrose
Fruit juice concentrate	Turbinado
Fructose	

Top Tips

MAKE good use of leftover food and you can create a quick and tasty omelette, stir-fry or soup without any fuss. Eggs add so much variety with omelettes and scrambles and add protein if you don't have meat available.

CHOPPING vegetables and meats into smaller pieces will reduce the cooking time.

IMPROVISE with your ingredients. If you don't have a particular ingredient in the cupboard, make a substitution for something similar, like kale instead of spinach.

KEEP an abundant supply of key ingredients as store cupboard essentials, such as tinned and frozen goods. Ready cooked pulses and beans, tinned tomatoes, tuna, sardines, stock (broth) and vegetables are a great resource and backup if your fridge is getting low. Yes, fresh is best but when needs must, frozen vegetables make great substitute without losing too many of nutrients. (Steer clear of soups, beans and sauces containing sugar).

MAKING larger portions of a meal than you require and stocking your freezer with them is a great way to ensure you can lay your hand on a quick dinner which can quickly be heated. Remember to label your freezer bags or containers so you can easily identify the contents.

PRE-PREPARED vegetables which have been washed, peeled and chopped ready for cooking are handy to have in the fridge although some find the taste is not quite the same.

READY cooked chicken and meat is available in the supermarket and means you can literally assemble a meal using salad leaves or add it to soups and stir-frys to save time.

MAKE a shopping list and stick to it. Think ahead to what you'd like to eat that week and make sure your fridge is stocked so you're not tempted by quick ready-meals or takeaways.

MASON jars are not only a great way of storing and transporting foods such as carrying salads to work, they can also be put in the microwave to warm up lunches.

Breakfast

Prawn & Basil Savoury Muffins

SERVES 1

208 calories per serving

Ingredients

25g (1oz) cooked peeled prawns (shrimps)

2 large eggs

1 teaspoon butter

1 teaspoon fresh basil leaves, chopped

Method

Crack the eggs into a large mug and beat them. Add in the butter, prawns (shrimps) and basil. Place the mug in a microwave and cook on full power for 30 seconds. Stir and return it to the microwave for another 30 seconds, stir and cook for another 30-60 seconds or until the egg is set. Serve it in the mug. Experiment with other ingredients, like chicken, bacon, beef, cheese and spring onions (scallions).

Smoked Salmon & Cream Cheese Scramble

Ingredients

75g (3oz) smoked salmon, finely chopped
50g (2oz) cream cheese
4 eggs
2 tablespoons crème fraîche
1 tablespoon butter
1 teaspoon chopped chives

SERVES 2

302
calories
per serving

Method

Crack the eggs into a bowl and whisk in the crème fraîche and chives. Heat the butter in a large frying pan and pour in the egg mixture. Continuously stir and cook the eggs until they begin to set. Stir in the cream cheese and smoked salmon and continue cooking until the eggs have set. Serve and eat immediately.

Parmesan & Herb Scramble

SERVES 1

204
calories
per serving

Ingredients

2 eggs

1 tablespoon crème fraîche

1 tablespoon grated Parmesan cheese

1 teaspoon fresh oregano, chopped

1 teaspoon fresh basil leaves, chopped

1 teaspoon butter

½ teaspoon mixed herbs (optional)

Method

Crack the eggs into a bowl, whisk them up. Add in the Parmesan cheese, crème fraîche, basil, oregano and mixed herbs (if using). Heat the butter in a frying pan. Pour in the egg mixture and stir constantly until the eggs are scrambled and set. Serve and enjoy.

Spiced Carrot Refresher

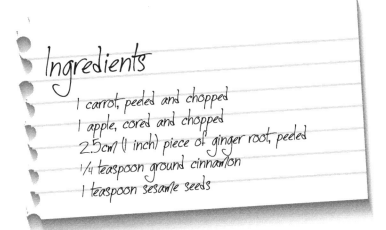

Ingredients

1 carrot, peeled and chopped
1 apple, cored and chopped
2.5cm (1 inch) piece of ginger root, peeled
1/4 teaspoon ground cinnamon
1 teaspoon sesame seeds

**SERVES
1**

117
calories
per serving

Method

Place all of the ingredients into a blender with enough water to cover them. Blitz until smooth. Serve and drink straight away.

Summer Berry Smoothie

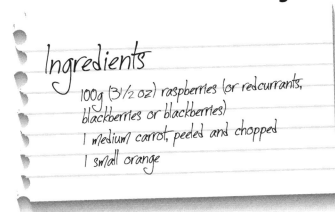

Ingredients

100g (3½ oz) raspberries (or redcurrants, blackberries or blackberries)
1 medium carrot, peeled and chopped
1 small orange

**SERVES
1**

95
calories
per serving

Method

Place all the ingredients into a blender with enough water to cover them and process until smooth. Serve and enjoy.

Coconut, Spinach & Lime Smoothie

Ingredients

1 small handful of fresh spinach leaves
Flesh of 1 small avocado,
50mls (2fl oz) coconut milk
Juice of 1 lime
Several ice cubes

**SERVES
1**

183
calories
per serving

Method

Place all of the ingredients into a food processor and add just enough water to cover them. Blitz until smooth and creamy. Serve and drink straight away.

Cleansing Cucumber Smoothie

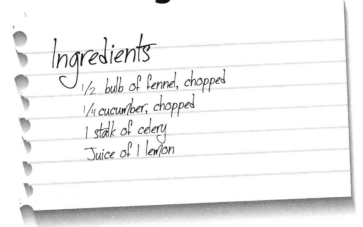

Ingredients

1/2 bulb of fennel, chopped
1/4 cucumber, chopped
1 stalk of celery
Juice of 1 lemon

**SERVES
1**

53
calories
per serving

Method

Place the fennel, cucumber and celery into a food processor or smoothie maker and add the lemon juice together with enough water to cover the ingredients. Process until smooth.

Minty Lime Shots

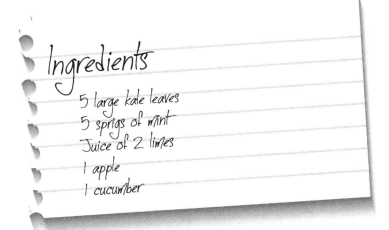

Ingredients

- 5 large kale leaves
- 5 sprigs of mint
- Juice of 2 limes
- 1 apple
- 1 cucumber

SERVES
1

152
calories
per serving

Method

Place the kale, limes, apples and cucumber into a juicer and process until you've extracted all the juice. Alternatively, use a blender and add sufficient water to cover the ingredients. Store in a bottle in the fridge and take healthy shots throughout the day or you can just drink it all straight away.

Chocolate Protein Shake

Ingredients

- 200mls (7fl oz) unsweetened almond milk
- 1 teaspoon 100% cocoa powder
- 1 teaspoon peanut butter
- 1/4 teaspoon stevia sweetener (optional)
- 2 teaspoons vanilla whey protein powder (sugar-free)
- Several ice cubes

SERVES
1

115
calories
per serving

Method

Place all of the ingredients into blender or food processor and blitz until smooth. Serve into a glass and enjoy!

Kiwi & Lettuce Shots

Ingredients

1 kiwi fruit, peeled
1 apple, cored
1/2 cos lettuce
Juice of 1/2 lemon

SERVES 1

91
calories
per serving

Method

Place all of the ingredients into a food processor with just enough water to cover them. Blitz until smooth. Pour the liquid into a glass bottle and keep it in the fridge, ready for you to have fresh shots throughout the day and a healthy drink between meals. Alternatively you can just drink it all straight away.

Pear Salad Smoothie

Ingredients

1 stalk of celery, roughly chopped
1/2 romaine lettuce, roughly chopped
1 large pear, cored
3 large sprigs of parsley

SERVES 1

83
calories
per serving

Method

Place all of the ingredients into a blender with sufficient water to cover them and blitz until smooth.

Avocado & Banana Smoothie

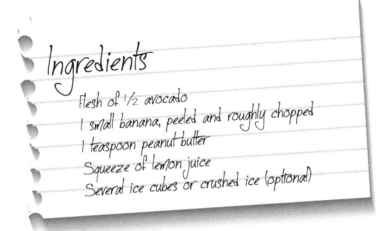

Ingredients

Flesh of ½ avocado
1 small banana, peeled and roughly chopped
1 teaspoon peanut butter
Squeeze of lemon juice
Several ice cubes or crushed ice (optional)

SERVES
1

233
calories
per serving

Method

Place all of the ingredients into a blender and blitz until smooth. If your blender doesn't tolerate ice you can just add a few cubes for serving.

Citrus Coconut Yogurt

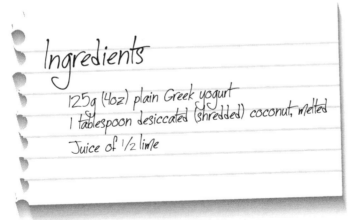

Ingredients

125g (4oz) plain Greek yogurt
1 tablespoon desiccated (shredded) coconut, melted
Juice of ½ lime

SERVES
1

258
calories
per serving

Method

Place the yogurt in a serving bowl and stir in the coconut oil until combined. Add in the coconut and lime juice and stir well. Serve into a bowl and eat straight away.

Macadamia & Chocolate Yogurt

Ingredients

100g (3½ oz) plain Greek yogurt
1 teaspoon 100% cocoa powder
6 macadamia nuts, chopped

SERVES 1

227 calories per serving

Method

Place the yogurt and cocoa powder into a bowl and stir until completely combined. Sprinkle the chopped nuts over the top. Serve and enjoy!

Raspberry & Flaxseed Swirl

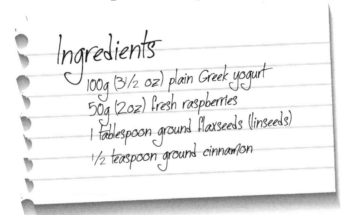

Ingredients

100g (3½ oz) plain Greek yogurt
50g (2oz) fresh raspberries
1 tablespoon ground flaxseeds (linseeds)
½ teaspoon ground cinnamon

SERVES 1

208 calories per serving

Method

Place the raspberries into blender or food processor and blitz to a smooth purée. Place the yogurt into a bowl and mix in the flaxseeds (linseeds) and cinnamon. Add the raspberry purée and partly stir it in leaving swirls in the yogurt. Serve and enjoy.

Ham & Egg Mug Muffin

Ingredients

2 eggs
1 slice of ham
1 teaspoon butter
1/4 teaspoon paprika

SERVES 1

197
calories
per serving

Method

Crack the eggs into a large mug and beat them. Add in the butter, ham and paprika and mix well. Place the mug in a microwave and cook on full power for 30 seconds. Stir and return it to the microwave for another 30 seconds, stir and cook for another 30-60 seconds or until the egg is set. Serve it in the mug. Experiment with other ingredients, like chicken, prawns, bacon, beef, cheese, spring onions (scallions) and herbs.

Thyme & Mushroom Omelette

196
calories
per serving

Ingredients

75g (3oz) mushrooms, chopped

2 eggs, beaten

1 small handful spinach leaves, chopped

1 tomato, cut into slices

1 teaspoon fresh thyme leaves, chopped

1 teaspoon olive oil

Method

Heat the olive oil in a saucepan, add the mushrooms and cook until softened. Remove them and set aside. Pour the beaten eggs into the frying pan and allow them to set. Transfer the omelette to a plate and fill it with the mushrooms, spinach, tomato and herbs then fold it over. Enjoy.

Low Carb Pancakes

Ingredients

50g (2oz) cream cheese
2 eggs
1 tablespoon butter
1/4 teaspoon cinnamon (optional)

SERVES
2

186
calories
per serving

Method

Place the eggs, cream cheese and cinnamon into a food processor and process until smooth. Heat the butter in a frying pan. Pour in half of the pancake batter and cook until the bubbles begin to appear in the mixture. Turn the pancake over and cook the other side until golden. Repeat for the remaining mixture. Serve with lemon juice, cream or bacon and sugar-free maple syrup.

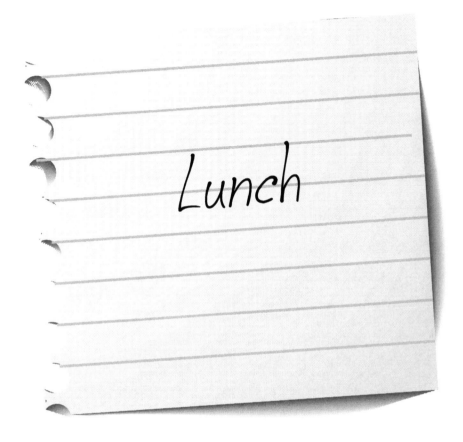

Lunch

Cheddar & Olive Frittata

Ingredients

- 25g (1oz) Cheddar cheese, grated (shredded)
- 25g (1oz) pitted black olives, halved
- 4 eggs
- 4 cherry tomatoes, halved
- 1 tablespoon fresh parsley, chopped
- 1 tablespoon fresh basil, chopped
- 2 teaspoons olive oil

SERVES 2

249
calories
per serving

Method

Whisk the eggs in a bowl and add in the parsley, basil, olives and tomatoes. Stir in the cheese and stir it. Heat the oil in a small frying pan and pour in the egg mixture. Cook until the egg mixture for around 3 minutes or until it completely sets. You can finish it off under a hot grill (broiler) if you wish. Gently remove it from the pan and cut it into two. You can easily double the quantity of ingredients and store the extra portions to be eaten cold.

Poached Eggs & Rocket

Ingredients

2 eggs
25g (1oz) fresh rocket (arugula)
1 teaspoon olive oil
Sea salt
Freshly ground black pepper

SERVES
1

178
calories
per serving

Method

Scatter the rocket (arugula) leaves onto a plate and drizzle the olive oil over them. Bring a shallow pan of water to the boil, add in the eggs and cook until the whites become firm. Serve the eggs on top of the rocket (arugula) and season with salt and pepper.

Tuna & Bean Salad

SERVES 2

352
calories
per serving

Ingredients

3 tablespoons lemon juice

1 tablespoon olive oil

1 clove garlic, chopped

250g (9oz) cannellini beans, drained and rinsed

250g (9oz) tinned tuna

1 onion, finely chopped

1 tablespoon fresh parsley, chopped

Method

Place the lemon juice, olive oil and garlic into a bowl and stir well. Add the cannellini beans, tuna, onion and parsley to the bowl and coat them in the oil mixture. Serve and eat straight away.

Greek Chicken Salad

Ingredients

75g (3oz) feta cheese, crumbled
50g (2oz) olives
2 tomatoes, chopped
2 cooked chicken breasts, chopped
1 small onion, chopped
1 romaine lettuce, chopped
½ cucumber, peeled and chopped
2 tablespoons apple cider vinegar
2 tablespoons extra-virgin olive oil
1 tablespoon fresh oregano, chopped
1 clove of garlic, chopped
Sea salt
Freshly ground black pepper

SERVES 2

482 calories per serving

Method

Place the oil, vinegar, oregano, garlic, salt and pepper into a bowl and mix well. Add the chicken, lettuce, cucumber, tomatoes, olives, onions and feta cheese and coat the ingredients in the oil mixture.

Chilli Taco-Style Salad

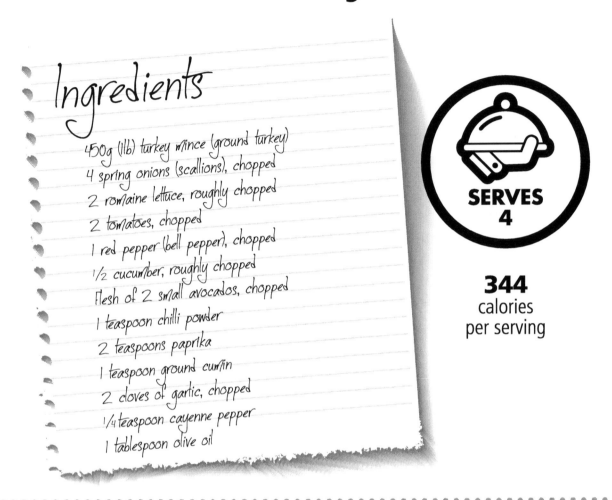

Ingredients

450g (1lb) turkey mince (ground turkey)
4 spring onions (scallions), chopped
2 romaine lettuce, roughly chopped
2 tomatoes, chopped
1 red pepper (bell pepper), chopped
1/2 cucumber, roughly chopped
Flesh of 2 small avocados, chopped
1 teaspoon chilli powder
2 teaspoons paprika
1 teaspoon ground cumin
2 cloves of garlic, chopped
1/4 teaspoon cayenne pepper
1 tablespoon olive oil

SERVES 4

344 calories per serving

Method

Heat the olive oil in a frying pan, add the turkey and cook until it's no longer pink. Sprinkle in the chilli, paprika, cumin, garlic and cayenne pepper and stir for 2 minutes or until the turkey is completely cooked. Scatter the lettuce, avocado, cucumber, tomato, pepper (bell pepper) and spring onions (scallions) onto plates. Spoon some of the chilli mixture on top of each salad. Serve and eat straight away.

Avocado, Coriander & Chicken Salad

Ingredients

2 cooked chicken breasts, chopped

2 avocados, peeled, de-stoned and chopped

1 tablespoon lime juice

3 spring onions (scallions) chopped

2 tablespoons fresh coriander (cilantro) leaves, chopped

2 tablespoons mayonnaise

SERVES 2

480 calories per serving

Method

Place the avocado flesh and lime juice into a bowl and mix well. Add the spring onions (scallions), chicken, mayonnaise and coriander (cilantro) and mix well. Serve with fresh green salad leaves and eat straight away.

Chicken & Blue Cheese Salad

SERVES 1

283 calories per serving

Ingredients

25g (1oz) blue cheese

4 spring onions (scallions), chopped

2 chicken breasts

2 large handfuls of salad leaves

2 tablespoons crème fraîche

1 tablespoon butter

1 teaspoon parsley

Method

Heat the butter in a frying pan, add the chicken and cook for 4 minutes then turn it over. Place the cheese on top of the chicken and cook until the chicken is completely cooked and the cheese has melted. Spoon the crème fraîche into the pan and stir until it warms through. Serve the salad leaves and spring onions (scallions) onto a plate. Place the chicken on the bed of salad and drizzle the sauce over the top. Sprinkle with parsley. Serve and eat immediately.

Serrano & Rocket Salad

Ingredients

150g (5oz) Serrano ham
1 large handful of spinach leaves
1 large handful of rocket (arugula leaves)
1 tablespoons olive oil
1 tablespoon apple cider vinegar
1 tablespoon fresh orange juice

SERVES 2

224
calories
per serving

Method

Pour the oil, vinegar and juice into a bowl and toss the spinach and rocket (arugula) leaves in the mixture. Serve the leaves onto plates and place the ham on top.

Lentil Soup

Ingredients

400g (14oz) tin of chopped tomatoes
350g (12oz) tinned green lentils (drained)
1 onion, chopped
1 teaspoon ground cumin
1 tablespoon olive oil
900mls (1½ pints) hot vegetable stock (broth)

**SERVES
4**

168
calories
per serving

Method

Heat the oil in a frying pan, add the onion and cook for 4 minutes. Add in the vegetable stock (broth), tomatoes, lentils and cumin and bring it to a simmer for around 5 minutes. Use a hand blender or food processor and blitz until smooth. Serve and enjoy.

Egg Drop Soup

Ingredients

250mls (8fl oz) chicken stock (broth)
1 teaspoon butter
1 egg
1/4 teaspoon chopped garlic
Pinch of chilli flakes
Sea salt

SERVES 1

120 calories per serving

Method

Heat the butter and chicken stock (broth) in a saucepan and bring it to the boil. Add in the garlic, chilli and salt and stir. Remove it from the heat. In a bowl, whisk the egg then pour it into the saucepan. Stir for around 2 minutes until the egg is cooked. Serve and eat immediately.

Asparagus Soup

Ingredients

375g (12oz) asparagus spears, tough ends removed

2 cloves of garlic, chopped

1 handful of spinach leaves

1 tablespoon butter

750mls (1½ pints) vegetable stock (broth)

SERVES 4

64 calories per serving

Method

Heat the butter in a saucepan, add the asparagus and garlic and cook for 4 minutes. Add in the spinach and vegetable stock (broth) and cook for 5 minutes. Using a hand blender or food processor blend the soup until smooth. Serve into bowls.

Chorizo Scramble

Ingredients

25g (1oz) chorizo sausage, chopped
25g (1oz) cheese, grated (shredded)
2 eggs, beaten
1 teaspoon butter

**SERVES
1**

375
calories
per serving

Method

Heat the butter in a frying pan and add in the chorizo. Cook for around 2 minutes. Pour in the beaten egg and stir, scrambling the eggs until completely cooked. Serve onto a plate and sprinkle with grated (shredded) cheese.

Creamy Chicken & Vegetable Soup

Ingredients

275g (10z) leftover roast chicken (or other cooked chicken)

3 tablespoons crème fraîche

2 carrots, chopped (or you can use leftovers if you have them)

1 onion, chopped

1 tablespoon olive oil

½ teaspoon dried mixed herbs

1 litre (1 ½ pints) vegetable stock (broth)

SERVES 4

188 calories per serving

Method

Heat the oil in a saucepan, add the onion, carrots and mixed herbs and cook for 4 minutes. Add in the stock (broth) and chicken and bring it to the boil. Reduce the heat and simmer for 4 minutes. Stir in the crème fraîche. Using a hand blender or food processor blitz HALF of the soup until smooth, then return it to the saucepan, making sure it is warmed through before serving.

Stilton & Celery Soup

Ingredients

450g (1lb) celery, chopped
150g (5oz) crème fraîche
75g (3oz) Stilton cheese
25g (1oz) butter
1 onion, chopped
600mls (1 pints) hot vegetable stock (broth)

SERVES 1

181
calories
per serving

Method

Heat the butter in a saucepan, add the onion and celery and cook for 1 minute. Pour in the stock (broth), bring to the boil then reduce the heat and simmer for around 8 minutes. Add in the crème fraîche and stir in the cheese until it has melted. Serve and eat straight away.

Parmesan Asparagus

Ingredients

200g (7oz) asparagus spears, trimmed
50g (2oz) Parmesan cheese, grated
1 tablespoon olive oil
Freshly ground black pepper

SERVES 2

191 calories per serving

Method

Heat the olive oil in a frying pan or griddle pan, add the asparagus and cook for around 4 minutes, turning occasionally. Sprinkle the parmesan cheese on top of the asparagus and cook for another couple of minutes or until the cheese has softened. Serve and season with black pepper. Eat straight away, either on its own or with a leafy green salad.

Red Chicory & Stilton Cheese Boats

SERVES 2

177 calories per serving

Ingredients

100g (3½ oz) chicory leaves, separated
75g (3oz) blue cheese, crumbled
1 teaspoon butter
Freshly ground black pepper

Method

Place the chicory leaves onto a baking sheet. Scatter the blue cheese into the chicory leaves and flake some butter into each one. Put them under a hot grill (broiler) and cook for around 4 minutes until the cheese has melted. Season with black pepper. Serve straight away.

Turkey & Chickpea Soup

Ingredients

300g (11oz) cooked turkey (leftovers are ideal), cut into strips

200g (6oz) tinned chickpeas (garbanzo beans), drained

1 onion, peeled and chopped

1 red pepper (bell pepper), de-seeded and chopped

2 teaspoons ground coriander (cilantro)

2 teaspoons butter

1 handful of fresh parsley, chopped

1 ½ litres (2¼ pints) vegetable stock (broth)

SERVES 4

234
calories
per serving

Method

Heat the butter in a large saucepan, add the onion and cook for 2 minutes. Add in the red pepper (bell pepper), ground coriander (cilantro) and stock (broth). Bring it to the boil, reduce the heat and simmer for around 6 minutes. Stir in the turkey, chickpeas (garbanzo beans) and parsley and warm it through. Serve into bowls and enjoy.

Cauliflower & Walnut Soup

Ingredients

450g (1lb) cauliflower, finely chopped
25g (1oz) butter
12 walnut halves, chopped
1 onion, chopped
600mls (1 ½ pints) hot water
125mls (4fl oz) crème fraîche
Sea salt
Black pepper
4 chopped walnuts for garnish

SERVES 4

184 calories per serving

Method

Heat the butter in a saucepan, add the cauliflower and onion and cook for 2 minutes, stirring continuously. Pour in the hot water, bring to the boil and cook for 10 minutes. Stir in the walnuts and crème fraîche. Using a food processor or hand blender, blitz the soup until smooth and creamy. Serve the soup with a sprinkle of chopped nuts.

Tomato & Pesto Soup

Ingredients

2 x 400g (14oz) tins of chopped tomatoes
2 cloves of garlic, chopped
2 teaspoons pesto sauce
1 teaspoon olive oil
360mls (12oz) vegetable stock (broth)
50mls (2oz) sour cream

SERVES 4

70 calories per serving

Method

Heat the oil in a large saucepan. Add the garlic and cook for 1 minute. Pour in the tinned tomatoes and vegetable stock (broth). Bring it to the boil then reduce the heat and simmer for 5 minutes. Using a hand blender or food processor whizz the soup until it becomes smooth. Serve the soup into bowls. Add in 2 teaspoons of pesto and a dollop of cream and swirl it with a spoon before serving.

Hummus With Carrot & Celery Crudités

Ingredients

1 carrot, cut into strips
6 celery stalks, cut into long strips
175g (6oz) tin of chickpeas (garbanzo beans), drained
2 cloves of garlic, crushed
1 tablespoon tahini (sesame seed paste)
Juice of 1 lemon
1 tablespoon olive oil
Sprinkling of paprika

SERVES 2

115 calories per serving

Method

Place the chickpeas (garbanzo beans), tahini (sesame seed paste), lemon juice and garlic into a blender and blitz until smooth Spoon the mixture into a serving bowl. Make a small well in the centre of the dip and pour in the olive oil and sprinkle on the paprika. Serve the carrot and celery sticks on a plate alongside the hummus.

Thai Curry Soup

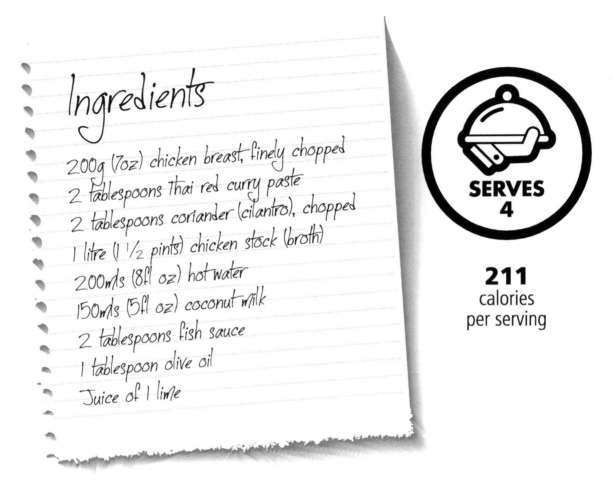

Ingredients

200g (7oz) chicken breast, finely chopped
2 tablespoons thai red curry paste
2 tablespoons coriander (cilantro), chopped
1 litre (1 ½ pints) chicken stock (broth)
200mls (8fl oz) hot water
150mls (5fl oz) coconut milk
2 tablespoons fish sauce
1 tablespoon olive oil
Juice of 1 lime

SERVES 4

211 calories per serving

Method

Heat the oil in a large saucepan. Add in the curry paste and cook for 1 minute. Add in the chicken and cook until it becomes opaque. Pour in the chicken stock (broth), water, fish sauce and coconut milk. Bring it to the boil, reduce the heat and simmer for 2 minutes making sure the chicken is completely cooked. Serve the soup into bowls and garnish with a sprinkling of fresh coriander (cilantro).

Quick Chicken & Mushroom Soup

Ingredients

200g (7oz) cooked chicken, chopped

4 medium mushrooms, finely chopped

4 spring onions (scallions) finely chopped

2 stalks of celery, chopped

1 tablespoon butter

1 tablespoon crème fraîche

500mls (1 pint) hot chicken stock (broth)

Sea salt

Freshly ground black pepper

SERVES 2

235 calories per serving

Method

Heat the butter in a saucepan, add the mushrooms, celery and spring onions (scallions) and cook for 1 minute. Pour in the chicken stock (broth) and chopped chicken. Bring it to a simmer and cook for 8-10 minutes. Stir in the crème fraîche and season the soup with salt and black pepper. Serve and eat straight away.

Chicken With Carrot & Courgette' Spaghetti'

SERVES 2

264 calories per serving

Ingredients

2 cooked chicken breasts, roughly chopped

2 carrots

2 courgettes (zucchinis)

1 tablespoon butter

1 tablespoon fresh parsley, chopped

Sea salt

Freshly ground black pepper

Method

Using a spiraliser, cut the carrots and courgettes (zucchinis) in strips. If you don't have a spiraliser, just use a vegetable peeler and cut into long then strips. Heat the butter in a frying pan, add the vegetables and cook for around 4 minutes. Add in the cooked chopped chicken and stir until it is warmed through. Season with salt and pepper. Sprinkle with parsley and serve.

Tuna With Lemon & Herb Dressing

SERVES 2

235
calories
per serving

Ingredients

2 tuna steaks (approx. 100g each)

2 large handfuls of salad leaves

1 teaspoon olive oil

FOR THE DRESSING:

25g (1oz) pitted green olives, chopped

1 small handful of fresh basil leaves, chopped

1 tablespoon olive oil

Freshly squeezed juice of 1 lemon

Method

Heat a teaspoon of olive oil in a griddle pan. Add the tuna steaks and cook on a high heat for 2-3 minutes on each side. Reduce the cooking time if you want them rare. Place the ingredients for the dressing into a bowl and combine them well. Scatter the salad leaves onto plates. Serve the tuna steaks with the dressing over the top.

Avocado & Devilled Eggs

Ingredients

2 large eggs, hard-boiled, halved
Flesh of 1/2 avocado
1 teaspoon goat's cheese
1 teaspoon olive oil
Pinch of salt
Sprinkle of cayenne pepper

**SERVES
1**

347
calories
per serving

Method

Gently scoop out the egg yolks and place them in a small bowl. Add the cheese, oil and a pinch of salt to the egg yolks and mix well. Stir in the avocado pieces to the egg mixture. Spoon the mixture onto the egg halves. Sprinkle with cayenne pepper and serve.

Beef & Coleslaw Rolls

Ingredients

3 slices cooked beef
3 teaspoons coleslaw

SERVES
1

230
calories
per serving

Method

Lay out the slices of beef. Spoon some coleslaw onto the end of one slice then roll it up. Repeat it for the remaining beef and coleslaw. Serve and eat straight away.

Dinner

Turkey Chilli

Ingredients

- 450g (1lb) minced turkey
- 100g (3½ oz) Cheddar cheese, grated (shredded)
- 200g (7oz) tin of black beans
- 400g (14oz) tin of chopped tomatoes
- 1 onion, peeled and chopped
- 3 garlic cloves, chopped
- 2 tablespoons tomato puree (paste)
- ½ teaspoon chilli powder
- 1 teaspoon olive oil

SERVES 4

363 calories per serving

Method

Heat the olive oil in a saucepan, add the garlic and onion and cook for 1 minute. Add in the turkey and cook it for 4 minutes, stirring occasionally to break up the meat. Add in the tomato puree (paste), chopped tomatoes, chilli and black beans. Place a lid on the saucepan and cook for around 6 minutes making sure the turkey is completely cooked. Serve into bowls and scatter some grated (shredded) cheese on top. You can also add guacamole and/or sour cream if you wish. Enjoy!

Mustard Crusted Cod

Ingredients

50g (2oz) ground almonds (almond meal/almond flour)

3 teaspoons Dijon mustard

2 cod fillets

1 teaspoon paprika

1/2 teaspoon garlic powder

1/4 teaspoon salt

1/2 teaspoon ground black pepper

2 teaspoons olive oil

1 tablespoon apple cider vinegar

SERVES 2

342 calories per serving

Method

Preheat the oven to 200C/400F. Place the almonds, paprika, garlic, salt and pepper into a bowl and mix well. Add in the mustard, olive oil and vinegar and mix well. Coat the cod fillets in the mixture. Place the fish on a baking dish and transfer it to the oven and cook for around 10-12 minutes or until the fish flakes easily. Serve the fish with green salad leaves. Enjoy.

Prawn & Chorizo Stir-Fry

Ingredients

450g (1lb) king prawns (shrimp), peeled
75g (3oz) chorizo sausage
1 red pepper (bell pepper), chopped
1 green pepper (bell pepper), chopped
1 onion, peeled and chopped
50mls (2fl oz) chicken stock (broth)
1 courgette (zucchini), chopped
2 cloves of garlic, chopped
½ teaspoon chilli powder
1 teaspoon olive oil
Sea salt
Freshly ground black pepper

SERVES 4

208 calories per serving

Method

Heat the oil in a frying pan, add the prawns (shrimps) and cook for 3 minutes. Remove and set aside. Place the onion and peppers into a saucepan with the garlic and courgette (zucchini) and cook for 3 minutes. Add in the chorizo sausage and return the prawns to the pan. Cook for 2 minutes. Pour in the hot stock (broth) and add in the chilli. Season with salt and pepper. Make sure the ingredients are completely cooked. Serve and enjoy.

Asparagus & Red Pepper Sauce

Ingredients

25g (1oz) ground almonds (almond meal/ almond flour)

14 stalks of asparagus, tough part of stalk removed

6 spring onions (scallions)

1 red pepper (bell pepper), halved and de-seeded

1/4 teaspoon chilli powder

2 tablespoons water

1 tablespoon olive oil

Juice of 1/2 lemon

Sea salt

SERVES 2

177 calories per serving

Method

Heat the oil in a griddle pan or frying pan. Add the asparagus and spring onions (scallions). Cook until they have softened, turning occasionally. In the meantime, place the red pepper (bell pepper), chilli powder, almonds, water and lemon juice into a blender and blitz until smooth. Serve the asparagus and spring onions onto plates and serve the sauce on the side.

Cajun Chicken & Green Peppers

Ingredients

2 handfuls of rocket (arugula) leaves

2 chicken breasts, chopped

2 cloves of garlic, chopped

1 green peppers (bell peppers)

1 onion, peeled and chopped

1 teaspoon Cajun seasoning

2 teaspoons olive oil

Sea salt

Freshly ground black

SERVES 2

241 calories per serving

Method

Place the chicken in a bowl and sprinkle on the Cajun seasoning making sure you coat it completely. Heat the oil in a large frying pan. Add the chicken and cook for around 3 minutes. Add in the onion, garlic, peppers and cook until the vegetables have softened. Scatter the rocket (arugula) on a plate and serve the chicken and vegetables on top. Season with salt and pepper. Eat straight away.

Celeriac Mash

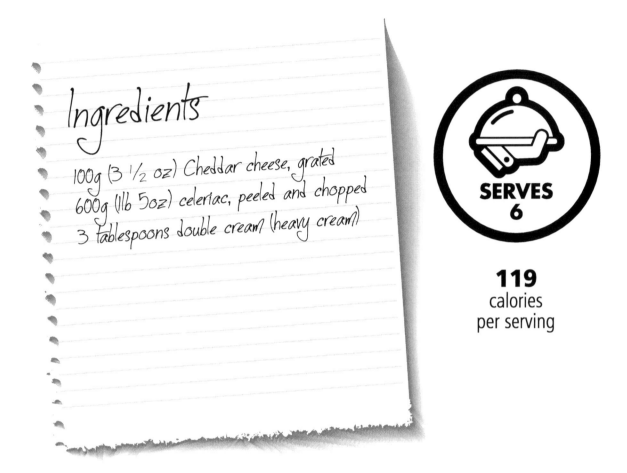

Ingredients

100g (3 ½ oz) Cheddar cheese, grated
600g (1lb 5oz) celeriac, peeled and chopped
3 tablespoons double cream (heavy cream)

SERVES
6

119
calories
per serving

Method

Place the celeriac into a saucepan, cover with hot water, bring it to the boil then reduce the heat and simmer for 10 minutes until tender. Drain off the water. Spoon the double cream (heavy cream) and butter onto the celeriac and mash it until smooth and creamy. Stir in the cheese. Serve as an accompaniment to meat, chicken and fish dishes as an alternative to potatoes.

Hazelnut Crusted Salmon

Ingredients

25g (1oz) hazelnuts
2 teaspoons Dijon mustard
2 medium salmon fillets
1 tablespoon fresh parsley
1 teaspoon olive oil

SERVES 2

387
calories
per serving

Method

Place the hazelnuts, mustard and parsley into a food processor and mix until soft. Heat the olive oil in a frying pan, add the salmon fillets and cook for 4 minutes on one side. Turn the salmon over and spoon the hazelnut mixture on top of the salmon fillets. Cook for around 3 minutes, or until the fish feels firm. In the meantime heat the grill (broiler). Finish the salmon off by placing it under the grill to finish off for around 2 minutes. Can be served alongside cauliflower mash or a green salad.

Lamb Chops & Aubergine

Ingredients

4 lamb chops

1 aubergine (eggplant) cut into 1cm lengthways slices

1 tablespoon pine nuts

1 tablespoon olive oil

Juice of 1/2 lemon

1/4 teaspoon paprika

Sea salt

**SERVES
2**

289
calories
per serving

Method

Heat a griddle pan or frying pan on a high heat. Lightly coat the aubergine (eggplant) slices with oil and sprinkle with sea salt. Place them on the pan and cook until they soften, turning once halfway through. In the meantime, place the lamb chops under a hot grill (broiler) and cook for around 4 minutes on each side or longer if you like lamb well done. Place the oil, lemon juice and paprika into a bowl and mix well. Serve the aubergine (eggplant) onto plates along with the lamb chops. Drizzle the dressing over the top and scatter on the pine nuts. Serve by itself or alongside a leafy salad.

Creamy Garlic Chicken

**SERVES
4**

283
calories
per serving

Ingredients

50g (2oz) Parmesan cheese, grated
(shredded)

50g (2oz) spinach, chopped

4 chicken breasts, sliced

2 cloves of garlic, chopped

200mls (7fl oz) crème fraîche

120mls (4fl oz) chicken stock (broth)

1 tablespoon olive oil

Method

Heat the oil in a frying pan, add the chicken and cook for around 5 minutes, stirring occasionally until it is cooked. Remove it and set aside, keeping it warm. Pour in the crème fraîche and add the garlic to the pan and stir. Add in the chicken stock (broth) and Parmesan cheese and stir until the mixture thickens. Scatter in the spinach and cook for around 2 minutes until it wilts. Return the chicken to the pan and make sure it is warmed through. Serve the chicken with the sauce. This goes really well with courgette 'spaghetti'.

Sea Bass
& Green Vegetables

**SERVES
2**

249
calories
per serving

Ingredients

75g (3oz) green beans, chopped
75g (3oz) asparagus, chopped
50g (2oz) broad beans
2 medium sea bass fillets
1 tablespoon olive oil
Freshly ground black pepper

Method

Heat the oil in a frying pan. Add the sea bass and cook them for about 3 minutes. Turn them over and cook for around 3-4 minutes. In the meantime, place the green beans, broad beans and asparagus into a steamer and cook for 5 minutes until they've softened. Serve the vegetables onto plates and add the fish on top. Season with pepper. Enjoy.

Prawn, Avocado & Cannellini Salad

Ingredients

- 200g (7oz) cooked king prawns (shrimps)
- 150g (5oz) tinned cannellini beans
- 2 large handfuls of spinach leaves
- 1 avocado, peeled, de-stoned and chopped
- 1 teaspoon fresh coriander (cilantro) leaves, chopped
- 1/2 cucumber, chopped
- 1/2 teaspoon chilli powder
- 1/2 teaspoon paprika
- Zest and juice of 1 lime
- 1 tablespoon olive oil

SERVES 2

373 calories per serving

Method

Place the prawns into a bowl and sprinkle on the paprika and mix well. Place the chilli, lime juice and zest and oil in a bowl and stir well. Add in the cannellini beans, avocado, cucumber and coriander (cilantro) and toss them in the dressing. Serve the spinach onto plates and add the tossed salad with the prawns on top

Tomato & Herb Chicken

Ingredients

400g (14oz) tinned chopped tomatoes
4 chicken breast fillets
2 cloves garlic, crushed
2 tablespoons tomato purée
1 onion, thinly sliced
1 small handful fresh basil leaves
1 teaspoon smoked paprika
1 teaspoon dried mixed herbs
1 tablespoon olive oil
¼ teaspoon salt
¼ teaspoon black pepper

SERVES 4

227 calories per serving

Method

Place the chicken in a bowl and sprinkle on the paprika, salt and pepper, coating it well. Heat the oil in a frying pan, add the chicken and brown it. Add in the garlic and onion and cook for 2 minutes. Add in the tomatoes and herbs. Bring it to the boil then simmer gently. Stir in the torn basil leaves and make sure the chicken is completely cooked before serving.

Creamy Turkey & Leeks

Ingredients

450g (1lb) turkey steaks, chopped
250g (9oz) button mushrooms
250g (9oz) leeks, chopped
200mls (7fl oz) chicken stock (broth)
200mls (7fl oz) crème fraîche
4 tablespoons chopped fresh parsley
1 tablespoon olive oil

SERVES 4

263 calories per serving

Method

Heat the olive oil in a large pan and add the turkey and mushrooms. Cook for 2 minutes, stirring constantly. Add in the leeks and stock (broth) and cook until the vegetables have softened and the turkey completely cooked. Add in the crème fraîche and warm it through. Sprinkle in the parsley before serving. This is delicious with cauliflower mash.

Quick Vegetable Curry

Ingredients

200g (7oz) small button mushrooms, chopped
175g (6oz) tofu, cubed
150g (5oz) green beans
3 teaspoons mild curry powder
1 tablespoon fresh coriander (cilantro)
1 teaspoon ground turmeric
1 teaspoon ground cumin
200mls (7fl oz) coconut milk

**SERVES
2**

305
calories
per serving

Method

Heat the coconut milk in a saucepan. Sprinkle in the curry powder, cumin and turmeric and stir until well combined. Add the mushrooms, green beans and tofu and stir well. Simmer for around 8 minutes until the vegetables are soft. Sprinkle with coriander (cilantro) and serve.

Chicken Nuggets

Ingredients

2 chicken breasts, cut into thick chunks
2 tablespoon Parmesan cheese, grated
2 tablespoons ground almonds
(almond meal/almond flour)
1 egg
1 tablespoon water

**SERVES
2**

325
calories
per serving

Method

Place the cheese, ground almonds (almond meal/almond flour) into a bowl and mix well. Mix in the egg and water and stir. Dip the chicken chunks into the almond mixture and coat them well. Heat a deep fat fryer to 190C/375F and add the chicken nuggets. Cook for around 5 minutes until golden and test them with a fork to check the chicken is cooked.

Pork Béarnaise

Ingredients

250g (8oz) pork steaks

2 large handfuls of green salad leaves

2 teaspoons mustard

1 tablespoon fresh parsley, chopped

1 teaspoon butter

2 tablespoons double cream (heavy cream)

2 tablespoons red wine vinegar

Sea salt

Freshly ground black pepper

SERVES 2

318 calories per serving

Method

Season the pork with salt and pepper. Heat the butter in a frying pan and add the steak. Cook for around 3 minutes on either side. Remove the pork, set aside and keep it warm. Reduce the heat and add in the vinegar, mustard and cream and stir well. Sprinkle in the parsley. Serve the pork onto a plate and pour the sauce over the top. Serve with green salad leaves.

Turkey Curry

Ingredients

450g (1lb) turkey breasts, finely chopped
5 cloves garlic, chopped
3 teaspoons medium curry powder
2 tablespoons fresh coriander (cilantro), finely chopped
1 onion, chopped
1 teaspoon turmeric powder
200mls (7fl oz) full-fat coconut milk
200mls (7fl oz) hot water
1 tablespoon olive oil

SERVES 4

303
calories
per serving

Method

Heat the olive oil in a saucepan, add the chopped onion and garlic and cook for 2 minutes. Add in the turkey and cook until it begins to turn white. Add the coconut milk, water, curry powder and turmeric. Bring it to the boil and stir in the coriander (cilantro) leaves. Serve with steamed vegetables or cauliflower rice.

Lemon Mustard Salmon & Lentils

Ingredients

- 250g (9oz) cooked Puy lentils
- 6 spring onions (scallions), chopped
- 2 salmon fillets
- 2 large tomatoes, chopped
- 1 small handful of basil leaves, chopped
- 2 large handfuls of rocket (arugula) leaves
- 2 teaspoons wholegrain mustard
- 1 teaspoon olive oil
- Zest and juice of 1 lemon

SERVES 2

399 calories per serving

Method

Place the lemon juice and mustard in a bowl and stir. Coat the salmon steaks in the mustard mixture. Place them under a hot grill (broiler) and cook for around 6 minutes turning once in between until the fish is cooked completely. Heat a frying pan, add in the lentils, spring onions (scallions) and tomatoes and cook for around 3 minutes or until warmed through. Stir in the basil leaves at the end of cooking. Serve the rocket (arugula) leaves onto plates and serve the lentils on top. Lay the cooked salmon on top of the lentils.

Basil & Lemon Swordfish Steaks

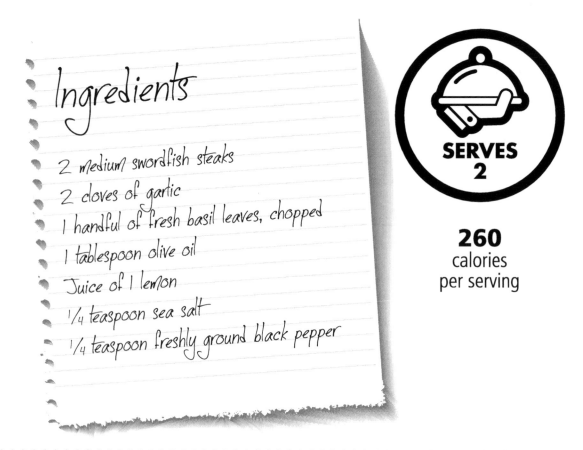

SERVES 2

260 calories per serving

Ingredients

2 medium swordfish steaks

2 cloves of garlic

1 handful of fresh basil leaves, chopped

1 tablespoon olive oil

Juice of 1 lemon

1/4 teaspoon sea salt

1/4 teaspoon freshly ground black pepper

Method

Place the lemon juice, olive oil, garlic, basil, salt and pepper into a large bowl. Place the fish on a plate and lightly coat the swordfish with 1-2 tablespoons of the lemon oil mixture. Heat a little olive oil in a hot pan and add the swordfish steaks. Cook for 3-4 minutes on each side and check that it's completely cooked. Serve onto plates with the remaining dressing.

Root Vegetable Stir-Fry

Ingredients

- 300g (11oz) Brussels sprouts, halved
- 2 large carrots, peeled and diced
- 1 large parsnip, peeled and diced
- 2 cloves of garlic
- 1 tablespoon olive oil
- 1 tablespoon fresh parsley, chopped
- 1/2 teaspoon ground nutmeg
- Sea salt
- Freshly ground black pepper

SERVES 2

161
calories
per serving

Method

Heat the oil in a wok or frying pan. Add in the Brussels sprouts, parsnip, carrots and garlic. Cook for around 5 minutes until the parsnip and carrots are tender. Sprinkle in the nutmeg and parsley. Season with salt and pepper before serving.

Quick Pesto Prawns

Ingredients

- 450g (1lb) king prawns, peeled
- 2 tablespoons pesto sauce
- 2 cloves of garlic, chopped
- 1 tablespoon olive oil

SERVES 4

154 calories per serving

Method

Spoon the pesto sauce into a large bowl. Add the garlic and mix well. Coat the prawns in the pesto sauce making sure they are completely covered. Heat the oil in a frying pan, add in the prawns and cook for about 5 minutes until they are completely pink through. Serve on their own or with a green salad on the side.

Scallops, Bacon & Garlic Butter

Ingredients

100g (4½ oz) large scallops, shelled
2 rashers of bacon, chopped
1 teaspoon fresh parsley, finely chopped
1 clove of garlic, finely chopped
2 teaspoons butter
Sea salt
Freshly ground black pepper

**SERVES
1**

315
calories
per serving

Method

Heat 1 teaspoon butter in a frying pan over a high heat. Add the scallops and cook for around 1 minute on either side until they are slightly golden. Transfer to a dish and keep warm. Add the bacon to the pan and cook for around 2 minutes. Add a teaspoon of butter and garlic and cook for around 1 minute until the butter has melted. Sprinkle in the parsley. Serve the scallops onto a plate and spoon the bacon and garlic butter on top. Season with salt and pepper.

Steak & Prawns With Garlic Sauce

SERVES 2

400 calories per serving

Ingredients

225g (7oz) peeled raw prawns (shrimps)
4 tablespoons crème fraîche
2 sirloin steaks (approx. 100g each)
2 tablespoons butter
1 tablespoon olive oil
3 cloves of garlic, chopped
Sea salt
Freshly ground black pepper

Method

Sprinkle salt on each side of the steaks. Heat the oil in a frying pan, add the steaks and cook for 3-4 minutes, (or longer if you like them well done) turning once. Remove them from the pan and set them aside and keep them warm. Heat the butter to the pan, add the prawns (shrimps) and crème fraîche and cook for until the prawns are completely pink. Season with salt and pepper. Serve the steaks onto plates and spoon the prawns and sauce over the top. Eat straight away.

Cauli Mash

Ingredients

1 medium cauliflower, broken into florets
1 tablespoon butter
2 tablespoons double cream (heavy cream)
Sea salt
Freshly ground black pepper

SERVES 6

69 calories per serving

Method

Place the cauliflower florets into a steamer and cook for around 10 minutes or until it becomes tender. Transfer the cauliflower to a food processor (or use a hand blender) and add in the butter, cream, salt and pepper. Blitz until it becomes smooth and creamy. Serve as a low carb alternative to mashed potatoes.

Desserts
& Snacks

Chocolate Chia Pudding

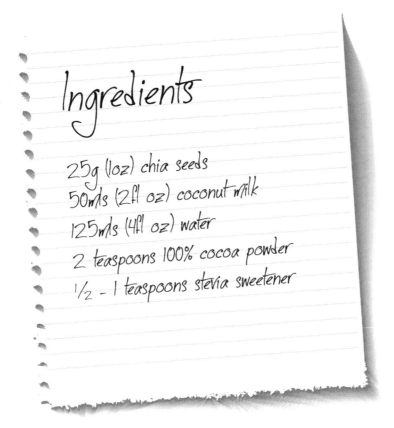

Ingredients

25g (1oz) chia seeds
50mls (2fl oz) coconut milk
125mls (4fl oz) water
2 teaspoons 100% cocoa powder
1/2 - 1 teaspoons stevia sweetener

SERVES 1

236
calories
per serving

Method

Place the chia seeds, cocoa powder and stevia into a bowl. Pour in the coconut milk and water and mix really well. Cover it and chill in the fridge for 20 minutes (or prepare and leave it overnight, ready for breakfast) then serve and enjoy.

Almond Mug Cake

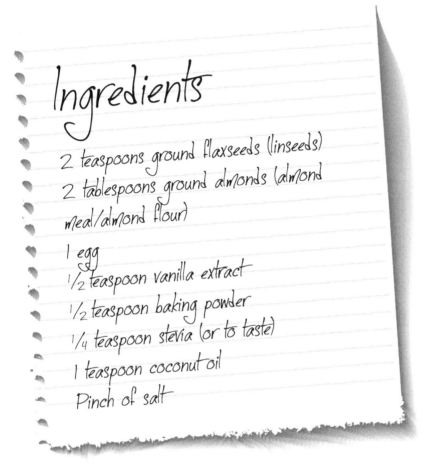

Ingredients

2 teaspoons ground flaxseeds (linseeds)
2 tablespoons ground almonds (almond meal/almond flour)
1 egg
1/2 teaspoon vanilla extract
1/2 teaspoon baking powder
1/4 teaspoon stevia (or to taste)
1 teaspoon coconut oil
Pinch of salt

**SERVES
1**

343
calories
per serving

Method

Place all the ingredients into a large mug or a microwaveable bowl and mix well. Cook in the microwave for 30 seconds. Remove it and stir. Return it to the microwave and cook for another 30 seconds, remove and return it to the microwave and cook for another 30 seconds. Chill in the fridge before serving.

Blueberry Mug Cheesecake

Ingredients

50g (2oz) cream cheese
25g (1oz) blueberries
1 egg
1/2 teaspoon vanilla extract
1/2 teaspoon stevia extract (or to taste)

SERVES 1

202
calories
per serving

Method

Place all the ingredients, except the blueberries, into a large mug or a microwaveable bowl and mix well. Cook in the microwave for 30 seconds. Remove it and stir in the blueberries. Return it to the microwave for another 30 seconds, remove and stir. Return it to the microwave for another 30 seconds. Chill in the fridge before serving.

Chocolate Mousse

**SERVES
4**

235
calories
per serving

Ingredients

100g (3½ oz) ricotta cheese

1 tablespoon butter

2 tablespoons 100% cocoa powder

2 teaspoon stevia (or to taste)

125mls (4fl oz) double cream (heavy cream)

Method

Place the butter and stevia into a bowl and mix well. Stir in the ricotta cheese and cocoa powder and mix thoroughly. Whip the cream until thick and fold it into the mixture. Spoon the mousse into dessert bowls and chill before serving.

Sweet Sugar-Free Popcorn

Ingredients

100g (3½ oz) unpopped popcorn
2 teaspoons butter
1 teaspoon stevia sweetener

**SERVES
2**

99
calories
per serving

Method

Place the butter/oil and stevia into a large saucepan and gently warm it while stirring. Turn the heat up high. Add the uncooked popcorn and place a lid on the saucepan. Cook for around 2-3 minutes or until all the corn has popped. Allow it to cool before serving.

Brazil Nut Truffles

Ingredients

100g (3½ oz) toasted coconut flakes
100g (3½ oz) Brazil nuts, chopped
2 teaspoons vanilla extract
2 tablespoons coconut oil

MAKES 16

92 calories each

Method

Place all of the ingredients into a blender and process until smooth and creamy. Add a little extra coconut oil if required. Divide the mixture into bite-size pieces and roll it into balls. Place the balls into small paper cake cases. Chill before serving.

Snowy Coconut Balls

Ingredients

125g (4oz) almond butter

75g (3oz) macadamia nuts, chopped

75g (3oz) desiccated (shredded) coconut

1 tablespoon tahini paste (sesame seed paste)

1 teaspoon vanilla extract

1 teaspoon stevia sweetener (or more to taste)

Extra coconut for coating

MAKES 24

80 calories each

Method

Place the coconut, tahini (sesame seed paste), almond butter, vanilla extract and chopped macadamia nuts into a bowl and combine them thoroughly. Stir in a teaspoon of stevia powder then taste to check the sweetness. Add a little more sweetener if you wish. Roll the mixture into balls. Scatter some desiccated (shredded) coconut on a plate and coat the balls in it. Keep them refrigerated until ready to use.

Sweet Chilli Peanuts

Ingredients

275g (10oz) unsalted peanuts
25g (1oz) butter
2 teaspoons stevia sweetener
½ teaspoon cayenne pepper
Pinch of salt

SERVES 10

174
calories
per serving

Method

Place the butter in a bowl and beat in the stevia, cayenne pepper and salt. Stir the peanuts into the butter mixture and spread them onto the baking sheet. Transfer them to the oven and cook at 200C/400F for 8-10 minutes, giving them a stir half-way through. Allow them to cool before serving.

Guacamole

Ingredients

2 ripe avocados
1 clove garlic
1 red chilli pepper, finely chopped
Juice of 1 lime
2 tablespoons fresh coriander leaves
(cilantro), chopped

SERVES 4

140 calories each

Method

Remove the stone from the avocados and scoop out the flesh. Combine all the ingredients in a bowl and mash together until smooth. Garnish with fresh coriander.

Parmesan Kale Chips

Ingredients

150g (5oz) kale leaves, chopped
25g (1oz) Parmesan cheese, finely grated
(shredded)
1/2 teaspoon salt
1/2 teaspoon garlic salt
1/2 teaspoon black pepper
1 tablespoon olive oil

**SERVES
4**

66
calories
per serving

Method

Preheat the oven to 200C/400F. Line a baking sheet with foil. Scatter the kale leaves on the baking sheet. Drizzle the oil over the top and sprinkle on the Parmesan cheese, garlic salt, oil, salt and black pepper. Place it in the oven and cook for 8-10 minutes.

Banana Frappuccino

Ingredients

1 frozen banana
175mls (6fl oz) almond milk
1 teaspoon instant coffee
1 teaspoon 100% cocoa powder
1/2-1 teaspoon stevia power (optional)

SERVES 1

143 calories each

Method

Toss all of the ingredients into a blender and blitz until smooth. Drink it straight away and enjoy!

Turmeric Chai Latte

Ingredients

- 1 vanilla bean
- 1 teaspoon turmeric
- 1/2 teaspoon ground ginger
- 1/2 teaspoon ground cinnamon
- 1 cardamom pod
- 360mls (12fl oz) water
- 25mls (1fl oz) whipping cream (heavy cream)
- Pinch of salt

**SERVES
1**

123
calories
per serving

Method

Place the cinnamon, ginger, cardamom, vanilla and salt in a saucepan along with the water and bring it to the boil. Reduce the heat and simmer until the mixture reduces to roughly half what you started with. Strain the liquid through a sieve and pour it into a heat-proof glass. Heat the cream in a saucepan and stir in the turmeric. Bring it to the boil. Pour the turmeric cream into the glass and stir well. Drink it straight away.

Fruit Infused Water

Ingredients

1 small orange, thinly sliced
1/2 fennel bulb, sliced
1-2 cups of ice cubes
2 litres (3 pints) of cold water

25
calories
per jug

Method

Fill a glass jug with water, add the fennel, orange and some ice and refrigerate it for 2-3 hours. This is a great replacement for sugary, fizzy drinks. You only need a small amount of fruit and you can experiment with some of these tasty combinations

Strawberry & Lime	Orange & Thyme
Cucumber & Fresh Mint	Lemon & Ginger
Raspberry & Orange	Raspberry & Basil
Pineapple & Mango	Pineapple, Cherry & Lemon
Apple, Ginger & Cinnamon	Mango & Lime
Apricot & Raspberry	Kiwi & Lemon
Cucumber & Lemon	Lime & Cucumber

You may also be interested in other titles by
Erin Rose Publishing
which are available in both paperback and ebook.

 Quick Start Guides

 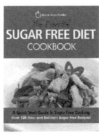   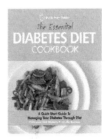

Books by Sophie Ryan
Erin Rose Publishing

30 Simple And Delicious Superfood Energy Balls And Bites
Recipes For Great Health and Wellbeing

Over 30 Easy And Delicious Superfood Energy Bars
Recipes To Boost Your Vitality

30 Simple And Tasty Energy Shots And Smoothies
To Power Up Your Health And Well-Being

Printed in Great Britain
by Amazon